Self Esteem:

The One Daily Habit

- To Boost It-

By

Maria Van Noord

© Copyright 2017 - All rights reserved.

The contents of this book may not be reproduced, duplicated or transmitted without direct written permission from the author.

Under no circumstances will any legal responsibility or blame be held against the publisher for any reparation, damages, or monetary loss due to the information herein, either directly or indirectly.

Legal Notice:

You cannot amend, distribute, sell, use, quote or paraphrase any part of the content within this book without the consent of the author.

Disclaimer Notice:

Please note the information contained within this document is for educational and entertainment purposes only. No warranties of any kind are expressed or implied. Readers acknowledge that the author is not engaging in the rendering of legal, financial, medical or professional advice. Please consult a licensed professional before attempting any techniques outlined in this book.

By reading this document, the reader agrees that under no circumstances are is the author responsible for any losses, direct or indirect, which are incurred as a result of the use of the information contained within this document, including, but not limited to, —errors, omissions, or inaccuracies.

Table of Contents

Table of Contents 5

Introduction 9

Chapter One: What Is Self-Esteem? 11

    What is self-esteem? 11

Chapter Two: Why Do You Need It? 18

    Good image 20

    Persistency 20

    Freedom 21

    Lesser pressure 21

    Taking a stance 21

    New challenges 22

    There is courage in accepting mistakes 22

    Becoming a leader 23

    Inspiration 23

    Coping 23

    Relationships 24

    Social gatherings 25

    Dating 26

    Sports 26

Chapter Three: Is It For The Lucky Few Or Can You Learn It? 28

    What is low self-esteem? 28

Negative work environment: 32

Subconscious: 32

Negative self-talk: 33

Change: 34

Past experiences: 34

Negative outlook: 35

Chapter Four: Components Of Self-Esteem 38

Chapter Five: Practical Tips 42

Step 1: It's time to stop your inner critic 44

Step 2: Better motivation habits 46

Step 3: Give yourself a pep talk 47

Step 4: Write down three things in the evening that you like about yourself 48

Step 5: Doing the right thing 49

Step 6: Stop chasing perfectionism 50

Step 7: Mistakes and failures should be dealt with positively 51

Step 8: Be kind towards others 53

Step 9: Trying something new 53

Step 10: Stop comparing 54

30-day plan 55

Daily Basis 55

Weekly basis 56

Bonus Chapter One: Affirmations 59

Affirmations for relationship 59

Affirmations for developing performance at school or university 60

Affirmations for sports 60

Affirmations for improving performance for workplace 60

Affirmations for improving your dating life 61

Affirmations for reaching goals 61

Conclusion 63

Introduction

I would like to thank you for purchasing this book "Self Esteem: Reach your life goals with Self-Love and Self-Confidence."

One of the most underrated ingredients for achieving success and happiness in life is self-esteem. Not many people give it a second thought, but your opinion of yourself can influence your life. Self-esteem is the regard you have for yourself. It is the opinion that you have the way you are. Knowingly or unknowingly, we all have formed views about ourselves. It could be based on what we think the world thinks of us or the manner in which we believe we should behave. All this unnecessary stress that we take tends to hurt our lives.

In this book, you will learn what self-esteem is all about, the importance of developing positive self-esteem, tips for identifying whether you have low self-esteem or not, and practical tips for improving your self-esteem. Not just that, you will also learn about positive affirmations and how they can help in improving your self-esteem. Replacing negative thoughts about yourself with positive ones can have a positive influence on your life. By consciously changing a few simple habits can help you in achieving the success you always dreamt of. So, are you ready to take control of your life once again? If yes, then let's get started without further ado.

Chapter One: What Is Self-Esteem?

"What lies behind us and what lies before we are tiny matters compared to what lies within us."
– Ralph Waldo Emerson

Self-esteem is also known as self-worth or self-respect, and it is an essential ingredient of success. If your self-esteem is lacking, then it can make you feel depressed and make you make self-destructive decisions. If you think that you aren't able to achieve the success that you want, then maybe stop looking for external factors and start examining yourself. Too little or too much of it can be a significant hurdle in your journey towards success. Self-esteem at either end of the spectrum is therefore undesirable, and you should be able to strike a balance. Having a realistic and positive view of yourself is considered to be desirable. However, what exactly is self-esteem? Where does it stem from and how does it influence our lives?

What is self-esteem?

In psychology, the term "self-esteem" is usually used for describing a person's general sense of personal value. Self-esteem refers to how much you value and appreciate yourself. It is a personal trait and involves a variety of opinions about yourself, such as the evaluation of your appearance, beliefs, emotions, feelings, and behavior. Self-esteem plays a significant role in your life. When your self-esteem is favorable, it has the power of motivating you and pushing you towards achieving your goals. However, low self-esteem can be a significant hurdle that can prevent you from attaining everything you ever dreamt of. Healthy self-esteem will help you in navigating life with a positive outlook towards it.

Different factors could influence your self-esteem. Genetic factors do play a role in shaping your overall personality, however, more often than not; our experiences form the basis for the development of our overall self-esteem. Those who tend to receive negative criticism from caregivers, family members, friends, and loved ones tend to struggle with low self-esteem. Other factors like your age, any disabilities, or other physical limitations, along with the kind of work you do can affect your self-esteem. Healthy self-esteem comes through in the form of confidence, your ability to say no, a positive outlook towards life, the ability to express yourself, and the ability to understand your strengths and weaknesses alike. Low self-esteem, on the other hand, manifests itself in the form of a negative outlook towards life, lack of confidence, the inability of expressing your desires, unnecessary feelings of shame and anxiety, the sense of inferiority, and everything else that's negative and undesirable. Self-esteem is the opinion you hold of yourself. If you hold yourself in good regard, then you will tend to have high self-esteem and low self-esteem if you don't have a good opinion of yourself. Your self-esteem usually depends on different questions:

Do you respect what you do and is your job worthwhile? Do you think that you are lucky? How do you perceive yourself? How do you usually feel about yourself? Do you ever criticize yourself? Do you often compare yourself to others and ignore your unique characteristics? What do you think about your social standing? Are you capable of making your own decisions?

Self-confidence refers to the level of confidence you have in yourself and your abilities. A self-confident person would do what they consider to be the right thing though others might criticize them. They would be willing to take risks, they would readily admit their mistakes and think of them as an opportunity to learn, would wait for others to congratulate them for what they have achieved, and they can accept compliments graciously. Whereas an individual whose self-confidence is low would tend to behave in a manner based on the opinions of others and not their own opinion. Such an individual wouldn't want to step outside their comfort zone or take any risks because of the fear of failure; they can't accept their mistakes and try to cover them up desperately before anyone can notice, brag about themselves, and they can't take compliments graciously and tend to dismiss them offhandedly. Self-confidence and self-esteem are closely related.

You can condition your mind not to indulge in unnecessary negative self-talk and by developing self-confidence; your self-esteem will improve as well. You can improve your self-confidence by doing a couple of simple things. Take some time out, and think of all that you have achieved, then list the ten best things that you have managed to achieve so far and pen them down. Now, place this list in a place where you can see it daily. Positive reinforcements can make you feel good about yourself.

The first step is to take a look at who you are and where you are in life. Look at the list of achievements you made in the previous step and introspect yourself by thinking about all the things that your friends consider are your strengths and weaknesses. Once you are through with this, think of all the opportunities available and the threats that you face. Make sure that you dwell and enjoy reading all your strengths. The next step would be to think about all that is important to you and what you want to achieve in your life. Once you have set the major goals, you need to devise a plan of action that will help you in achieving those goals.

"A healthy self-love means we have no compulsion to justify to ourselves or others why we take vacations, why we sleep late, why we buy new shoes, why we spoil ourselves from time to time. We feel comfortable doing things that add quality and beauty to life."

– Andrew Matthews

Self-compassion refers to the compassion with which you treat yourself, the love and warmth you show yourself whenever you stumble or fall. Do you react harshly towards yourself or are you compassionate? Would you extend the same compassion that would show your friend towards yourself?

Chapter Two: Why Do You Need It?

Until you value yourself, you won't value your time. Until you value your time, you will not do anything with it. "
– M. Scott Peck

Most people believe that building self-esteem is for their good. Positive self-esteem does make you more confident while facing life; it will make you happier, and let you lead a better life as well. However, the benefits of self-esteem go above and beyond that. Positive self-esteem improves your level of self-confidence. With self-confidence comes self-respect, which in turn will make others respect you as well. Once people start recognizing you, the equation you share with them will improve, and all this will make you happier. Low self-esteem on the other hand often leads to depression, anxiety, low self-confidence, and unhappiness with yourself and all those around you. Low self-esteem will make you doubt yourself, reduce your self-confidence, and prevent you from achieving all that you ever wanted.

Most people don't like being around those with low self-esteem because they tend to dampen the spirits of those around them as well. The emotions we feel are projected towards those around us. So, happy feelings radiate happiness, and the negative ones radiate negativity. Individuals with positive self-esteem are capable of accepting themselves positively. They can love and respect themselves, and this helps them in forming positive relations with those around them. Positive self-esteem provides the confidence and the ability to work towards achieving the goals you have established for yourself. Working on developing your self-esteem isn't a selfish goal and it, in fact, helps in improving your well-being as well as that of those around you.

In the world that we live in, money and stature tend to be the parameters of measuring one's success. The society we live in forces most of us to mold themselves into something that they are not. All this pressure leads to the depletion of self-esteem and causes the individual to lose confidence. So, people slowly resign to the fact that they aren't good enough or that they don't belong in the society they live in. Low self-esteem might not seem like a big deal for some, however, for most people, it is equivalent to a devastating disease. Individuals who suffer from low self-esteem tend to become loners and tend to avoid all sorts of personal relationships and interactions with those around them. Others are affected to the extent where they give up on their dreams. Developing positive self-esteem can help you in reaping the benefits that are mentioned in this section.

It is quite tricky to assess those who are close to us, but it needs to be done. You should take note of those who bring you down and those who bring in some positivity into your life. Yes, it is a difficult task, but you need to do this to get away from those who have a negative impact on your life. These people could be your acquaintances, friends, or even family members. If you are interested in developing your self-esteem, then you should work on surrounding yourself with those who bring in some positivity. Positive energy will rub off on you, and you will feel better about yourself. Stop thinking that your life is about being happy or sad. Your life is about making such choices that will make you happy or sad.

Good image

All those who have positive self-esteem tend to dress confidently. A man who wants to look confident would dress sharply. When you feel good about yourself, this will be automatically projected in the way you dress and behave. Not just that, it would have a favorable impact on your body language as well.

Persistency

Most people tend to think of failure as a significant setback. Persistency is a trait that helps people in achieving success, regardless of the number of times they fail. The "will" to keep trying and to stand up even after falling is considered to be an opportunity to improve themselves. A confident person would never boast that they are right, and they aren't scared of making mistakes. A person with positive self-esteem would think of every experience- positive and negative ones, as a chance to learn and improve.

Freedom

High self-esteem will allow you to drop all pretenses and it will enable you to be yourself without any obstructions. Individuals who are capable of being themselves are often happier and successful in life.

Lesser pressure

Since you are free to drop all the pretenses and be yourself without having to be someone else, the stress that they experience is less. Less stress means that they can divert all their energies towards achieving their goals instead of focusing on unnecessary things. Once they do this, they can start working on improving themselves. Only when you learn to be content with yourself, will you learn to be happy.

Taking a stance

A confident person will always have strong beliefs about things that they feel strongly about. Those who lack confidence and self-esteem aren't capable of defending their views or taking a stance. They tend to give in to what others think and never express their real opinions. An individual with positive self-esteem will be able to deliver his or her views without worrying about ridicule or rejection from others. Fear can prevent you from achieving your goals and a person with high self-esteem is aware of it.

New challenges

With every single opportunity that comes your way, there are different challenges that you will need to face as well. All those who have low self-esteem tend to hide in their comfort zone, whereas a person with high self-esteem would want to step forward and face the challenge head-on. Such a person wouldn't mind stepping out of their comfort zone. A successful person knows that the first step towards success is to step out of your comfort zone and embrace different challenges that come along your way.

There is courage in accepting mistakes

Like mentioned earlier, those who have high self-esteem don't think of their mistakes as the loss. A mistake for them is a chance to learn and improve themselves. Instead of feeling bad for themselves, those who are confident, will pick themselves up, dust themselves off, and prepare themselves for the next challenge.

Becoming a leader

Having high self-esteem is one of the essential qualities that a leader should possess. Leaders should have self-confidence since the choices they make have the power of affecting the entire team. A leader who is caught unawares or who isn't ready to take responsibility immediately is not just a liability to themselves, but for the team as well.

Inspiration

Those who have positive self-esteem tend to have good leadership qualities that help in inspiring all those who are around them as well. Having a good leader is quite essential, and they are capable of influencing the productivity of all those who are around them as well.

Coping

There will always be a certain situation that is hard to recover from. Individuals who have low self-esteem will need longer to heal than the ones who have healthy self-esteem. Those who aren't confident cannot improve, and they will always hesitate from taking the first step. All those who have confidence will keep going, take the necessary steps for improving themselves, and make sure that they never find themselves in a similar situation ever again.

Have you ever heard the saying "too much of a good thing is bad?" well, it stands true when it comes to self-esteem as well. Having healthy self-esteem is a good thing, and too much of it will just make you seem arrogant and almost pompous. High self-esteem often treads the fine line between confidence and arrogance, and along the way that line gets blurry. If a person acts rude and isn't respectful towards others, then such person would be considered to be arrogant and not as someone who has positive self-esteem. All those individuals who fall into this category are quite tricky to confront, and this difficulty stems from the fact that these people have developed a strong sense of immunity towards the opinions that others hold.

Relationships

Self-esteem plays a significant role in your relationships. If you aren't capable of appreciating, loving, and accepting yourself, it is likely that no one else will. You might end up settling for less than you deserve. The connection or the bond that you have formed with your partner is a superficial one. Low self-esteem will prevent you from having any positive expectations and will lead to the development of negative expectations about your relationship. You might start thinking that you don't deserve to have a happy, meaningful, and long-lasting relationship. Your insecurities will make you clingy and unreasonably jealous. You will need constant reassurance from your partner, and this can drive your partner away. Lastly, you are perhaps with your partner for all the wrong reasons, and you might be in a relationship because you think you will never find anyone else.

Social gatherings

Your self-esteem plays a significant role in the way you behave in a social setting. If you are comfortable in your skin, only then will you be able to mingle freely with others. If not, you will just feel like an outsider. If you are confident about yourself, others will want to talk to you. Before anything is said verbally, you have the opportunity to make use of your body language to give the other person an indication that you are a friendly and approachable person. Inviting body language would include simple things like a pleasant smile and not closing yourself off by crossing your arms or even scowling. There is another way in which you can seem friendly while starting a conversation. If you have low self-esteem, then your body language will indicate the same. Your mental state often manifests itself in your body language. It is next to impossible for you to imagine yourself in a scenario where you are picking up a random conversation with a stranger. You don't like initiating small talk with the salesperson at a store or anyone else for that matter. Once you overcome your shyness and have developed your self-esteem, small talk will come naturally to you. You can project self-esteem by making direct eye contact and also by smiling. Not just this, but also your posture, gestures and the way you carry yourself to tell others and your nervous system how confident you are.

Dating

Low self-confidence can wreak havoc on your dating life. Your inability of letting go of the past can ruin any prospective relationship. The constant reassurances that you need, will make you come across as being needy and clingy. The behavior of this sort can scare anyone away.

Sports

Sports can help in improving your self-image. Sports, especially team sports will make you feel more comfortable in a public setting. Not just that, it will promote healthy competition which will, in turn, lead to your overall development. Also, sports help in maintaining your physical health and fitness. Improved body image helps in improving your self-esteem as well.

Having positive self-esteem is quintessential if you want to get ahead in life. If you want to be successful and achieve the goals you have set for yourself, then you need to be sure of yourself and your abilities. You should hold yourself in high regard. If you do not respect and value yourself, you certainly cannot expect anyone else to do the same. If you want to reap all the benefits that were discussed in this chapter, then you should start developing healthy self-esteem.

Chapter Three: Is It For The Lucky Few Or Can You Learn It?

Well, do you feel that only a few are blessed with positive self-esteem? If that's what you think, then you are mistaken! Like any other personality trait, self-esteem can be developed too. If you feel that you are lagging in it, then you can start working on improving it. However, before you learn about that, you need to understand what low self-esteem is and the causes of it.

What is low self-esteem?

A reduced image of yourself leads to low self-esteem. Self-image is your perception of yourself, the way you see yourself. Do you think you are dependable, hardworking, friendly, or an honest person? Do you feel comfortable with the way you are? Do you like what you see when you look in the mirror? Do you believe that others look, and dress better than you do? Low self-esteem can be caused due to other aspects like your job. For instance, do you like your job? Does your work make you happy and does it add any value to your life? Do others respect you? Low self-esteem stems from negative thinking and its criticisms that others make of you. Do you feel bogged down by the criticism you receive from others? Do you think that you lose confidence because of all this?

On the other hand, high self-esteem is precisely the opposite of everything that's been mentioned above. You will feel confident, motivated, and have a positive outlook towards life when you have a healthy self-esteem. We all tend to have a personal self-image or an opinion about ourselves; our perception of strengths and weaknesses and these beliefs are formed from an early age. Our self-image plays a significant role in our life, our interactions with others, and everything else that we do in our life. Your belief in yourself affects your self-esteem. Self-esteem is nothing more than the set of feelings you have about yourself. People lacking in self-esteem cannot see their worth, and they don't believe in their abilities. They tend to think that they are somehow flawed and are inferior to those around them. It isn't always easy to figure out which category you fall under. Here are a couple of thoughts and behaviors that are usually associated with those who have low self-esteem.

Whenever someone compliments you, are you comfortable accepting it? Do you feel like you deserve the compliment, or do you say something to brush it off? You should accept compliments willingly. You don't have to minimize your expression of elation from others. Instead of brushing away complements you can graciously accept them. Giving is an important aspect of life, and so is receiving. When you accept a compliment willingly and graciously, you give others an opportunity to experience the happiness of giving. It shows not just your modesty but also your confidence in yourself. Can you express your opinion freely and trust it? Whenever you have something important to say, do you take your turn and express yourself? Can you maintain eye contact with others while expressing yourself or do you always look down? Whenever you walk into a room for the first time, do you sit in the front seats? Usually, all those who opt to sit on the edge are the ones who don't want to be noticed, and this behavior is associated with all those who have low self-esteem. Are you a good judge of yourself? Are you capable of taking negative criticism from those around you and are you capable of accepting your mistakes? Can you work on improving yourself based on the criticism you receive, or do you get defensive or depressed? Do you understand that a portion of the comments you receive from someone isn't representative of the general opinion that others have of you? Can you accept your uniqueness? You might wish to be taller, slimmer, more outgoing, and less impulsive. However, whenever you ask yourself "Who am I?" Do you have an answer to it that takes into consideration your uniqueness? Even after a tiring day, can you maintain good body posture, or do you slouch? Would you consider yourself to be optimistic or pessimistic? Do you like wearing clothes that you want or are your choices influenced by what others think of you? Do you do things for your satisfaction or because someone else has asked you to do a particular job?

Take some time out, and answer the questions mentioned above honestly. Everyone would have faced some instance or another in their life that reduced their self-esteem. It is quite natural. However, it is essential to build it back and not let your self-esteem plummet further. Like any other personality trait, even self-esteem can be improved.

Barriers to self-esteem

> *"Too many people overvalue what they are not and undervalue what they are."*
>
> *– Malcolm S. Forbes*

Well, have you ever seen babies? Don't they all seem confident? Yes, they do. We are all born confident, and our experiences can enhance or diminish these feelings. A child is always eager to learn more and will keep trying even if the child fails. So, where does that will, and motivation disappear? It might feel like there are plenty of barriers to self-esteem. However, if you are interested in developing yourself, then the first that you should work on is improving your self-esteem. Until you do this, it wouldn't be easy for you to assess and achieve your goals. Low self-esteem can also prevent you from seeing what your goals are. Think of your life as an empty dartboard, and everyone around you has the potential of becoming a dart that can potentially damage your life at one point or another. Those darts are bound to hurt your self-esteem in ways you cannot even consciously comprehend. So, what are the darts that you should be aware of and avoid? Let us take a look at the different things that act as barriers to your self-esteem.

Negative work environment:

Have you ever heard the phrase "dog eat dog," where everyone is fighting just to get ahead of the other? Well, beware of it because this is where all those who aren't appreciative tend to thrive. In such a scenario, no one is going to appreciating anyone else. Stay away from such a negative environment. It will just bring you down, and it will shatter your self-esteem as well. Don't get involved in power games or other negative behaviors like manipulation that will make you think less about yourself. Compete with others on your terms, if you have to compete.

Subconscious:

Our mind works consciously and subconsciously as well. Your conscious mind is responsible for all the actions you do knowingly- the things that require active thought. However, most of our mind works subconsciously. Your subconscious can influence you a great deal. If you think positively about yourself, then you will feel good about yourself. However, any deep-seated feelings of inadequacy, incompetence, or anything negative will make you feel poorly about yourself. Your self-esteem will take a hit, and you wouldn't even realize it.

Your thoughts create your reality, and by changing the way you think, you can recreate your reality as well. It isn't that difficult. You need to condition your mind to think positively. Things don't necessarily go as you planned for them and you might or might not achieve everything you have set out to do. Failures and setbacks are common. However, what matters is your ability to bounce back.

Negative self-talk:

We all have a tiny voice in our head that keeps saying we aren't good enough, that we might fail, or we cannot achieve our goals. It is quite normal, and everyone thinks such thoughts. However, when you start indulging in too much negative self-talk, you are setting yourself up for failure. If you don't believe in yourself, it is highly unlikely that someone else would. Try to change this pattern and indulge in some positive self-talk. If you tell yourself, you are good at what you do, and you deserve to attain your goals, after a while, you will start believing it as well. Whenever you hear negative self-talk, stop it, immediately. All such talk does is make you feel depressed and disappointed with yourself. Making use of powerful imagery will also help you understand what you will experience and feel when you have managed to achieve your goals, and this is sufficient motivation to keep on pushing.

The behavior of others: You will come across all sorts of negative people in your life, from gossipmongers to naggers, complainers and backstabbers. It all depends on whether you let their negativity get to you or not. Negative behavior will damage your self-esteem and self-development. Learn to identify such behavior and avoid it.

Change:

Don't resist change. Change is a natural process, and there will be stagnation if there isn't any change. Go with the flow and don't stress too much about it. Think of change as an opportunity to do something better.

Past experiences:

Your past should be a learning experience for you, but it shouldn't dictate the way you behave. If you got hurt in the past, learn from it and don't let that fear take hold of you. Each failure and mistake are a learning opportunity and treat it as such. Don't let your past experiences ruin your future for you. If you grew up hearing that you weren't good enough, how can you possibly develop positive self-esteem as an adult? If you were criticized regardless of how hard you worked and tried, it does get difficult to feel confident about yourself. If you don't feel comfortable in your skin, then you should think about the reasons that make you feel so. It can be quite painful when the authority figures you were exposed to while growing up were disapproving. You think it is difficult to keep up your motivation levels, to strive for more than what you have, and imagine that you deserved more when your primary caregivers or parents didn't pay much attention to you or acknowledge your achievements. A scenario like this will make you feel dejected and unrecognized, and these feelings probably followed you into adulthood as well.

Negative outlook:

Don't get consumed by all the negativities that exist in this world. A negative outlook towards life will always prevent you from seeing all the good that is there in you and around you.

"Be faithful to that which exists within yourself."

– André Gide

What is your take on self-love? More importantly, do you love yourself? If you have any difficulty feeling, expressing, and accepting self-appreciation, then you should think about developing self-love. Self-love and self-esteem are interwoven concepts, and one cannot exist without the other. You probably spent a lot of your time and effort demanding perfection from yourself. When you start chasing perfection, you set impossibly hard standards of success and more often than not, you will fall short regardless of how hard you try.

The feeling of "I'm not good enough" can stop you from making the most of the opportunities that come along your way. Unknowingly, you are sabotaging your life, relationships, and career. For instance, think of a situation where your loved one comes to you about something that's troubling them. Your friend tells you that he or she feels stuck and like a failure, what would you say? Would you react kindly to them? You probably would, and you would try to make them feel better about themselves. So, when it comes to you, why don't you extend the same compassion towards yourself? When you are kind to yourself, and when you love yourself, your self-esteem will improve.

Your childhood, upbringing, and several other genetic traits also contribute to the way you are. However, don't ever think that your genetics determine who you are. You have the power of becoming better and of changing yourself, provided you want to. The first step in improving your self-esteem is to understand what self-esteem is all about and determine your level of self-esteem. By answering the questions mentioned in this chapter and by examining and monitoring your feelings towards yourself, you would be able to decide on your level of self-confidence.

Chapter Four: Components Of Self-Esteem

"Be faithful to that which exists within yourself."
– André Gide

In a general sense, self-esteem is related to how we cope with the happenings in our lives and the acknowledgment of our inherent right to happiness. Our self-esteem partly depends upon the approval of others and partly from the sense that we have behaved reasonably and that we are competent at what we do. It is a popular belief that not just positive thinking can build self-confidence but also use affirmations.

Self-esteem comprises of two parts: the degree to which you like yourself and the extent to which you think you are competent. What exactly is self-esteem made up of? Whenever someone is talking about self-esteem, they are talking about the general view a person has about himself. However, self-esteem is made up of two things.

The first aspect is regarding the extent to which people tend to like themselves. That is, it refers to the attitude that people have towards themselves. A couple of affirmations that showcase a higher level of this aspect of self-esteem are "I feel great about who I am," "I am quite comfortable with myself," and "I hold myself in positive regard." This attitude is referred to as self-worth. Whenever you see yourself improving a skill and achieving goals that are related to those skills, you gain a sense of self-efficacy. It is the confidence you have in yourself that you are capable of succeeding if you learn and put in some hard work. It is the type of confidence that enables individuals to take up challenges even when faced with difficulties.

The second component is regarding the competency or the capability of a person. It is known as personal competence, and it is entirely different from self-worth. Self-worth depends on your opinion of your worthiness whereas personal competence is the extent to which you think you are capable of. Affirmations that project this attitude are "I'm very creative," "I am quite good at the different thing," and "I am effective and efficient in the way I work."

The coexistence of these two components is the main reason why some might think they are fond of themselves but would simultaneously think that they aren't useful. At times, a person might be quite capable and successful, and yet isn't fond of himself or herself. Self-esteem differs from self-confidence and self-awareness. Self-awareness refers to a person's awareness of his or her capabilities and self-confidence refers to the degree of confidence a person has in himself or herself

> *"Whatever course you decide upon, there is always someone to tell you that you are wrong. There are always difficulties arising, which tempt you to believe that your critics are right. To map out a course of action and follow it to an end requires courage."*
>
> *– Ralph Waldo Emerson*

Your attitude has a significant influence on your self-esteem. There are different choices that you have to make daily that can help or even hurt your self-esteem. The kind of choices you make is directly related to the attitude you possess. Your view can affect your self-esteem in the following ways.

Your attitude defines the way you look at yourself. Having a positive attitude doesn't necessarily mean that your self-esteem will increase, but it certainly does go a long way in helping improve your self-esteem. If you start adopting a positive outlook on your life and things in general and start thinking about yourself a little positively, you will start feeling good about yourself. Quite often, your attitude reflects how you feel about yourself. If your self-esteem is low, then you will find it difficult to meet new people. Also, your attitude towards a given situation will help in determining whether you will be able to overcome your shyness and awkwardness when it comes to new people or not. The more positive your outlook is towards meeting new people, the easier it will be for you to overcome your fear and this, in turn, helps in improving your self-esteem. When you can step out of your comfort zone, your sense of self-esteem will increase.

Chapter Five: Practical Tips

"No one can make you feel inferior without your consent."
– Eleanor Roosevelt

There is nothing more important than the way you feel about yourself, and how considerate you are towards yourself. Holding yourself without being overconfident and loving yourself for who you are amongst those things that people these days seem to have forgotten about. Self-esteem is an essential trait, but why is it essential to build and maintain positive self-esteem?

When you love and accept yourself for being yourself, that's when life becomes easy. You will no longer make mountains out of molehills, and you will finally stop beating yourself up for the simple mistakes you make. Learning to accept yourself, the good and the bad will help you in feeling lighter, and life does get easier when you do this. Don't set impossibly tricky standards for yourself. When you finally like yourself and when your opinion of yourself improves, you will stop trying to earn validation and attention from those who are around you. When you stop living your life for someone else's approval, you will finally start living for yourself. Doing this will lend you some sense of inner stability that will prevent you from becoming needy and dependent on others for your happiness. You will stop trying to sabotage yourself. You are your worst critic, and by improving your self-esteem, you will stop being too hard on yourself, and you will start feeling that you deserve good things in life. So, you will start making a conscious effort to achieve what you want and the motivation you need, will also automatically come to you. You will become aware of any form of negative behavior that harms you. You will feel more stable, and you will be better equipped at dealing with tough times. Instead of being a needy receiver all the time, you will be able to become a giver. It will become more comfortable to be with you, and all the drama, fights, or arguments will also reduce. The most critical and obvious benefit is that you will start feeling happier. Your happiness is no longer dependent on someone else's opinion, but it is in your hands, and you know it. How, many times have you told yourself "just this once"? Most of us have convinced ourselves that we are capable of breaking our own rules. We will always find reasons to justify these small choices we make. None of these things feel like a significant decision initially. However, over a period, these things end up forming a part of the bigger picture. Human beings are good at sabotaging their selves. People tend to behave in a manner that goes against their goals or their ideals. The gap between what you do and what you should be doing should be as small as possible. The smaller this gap is, the happier you will be in life. Giving 100% commitment is easier than giving 98%. When you have committed yourself fully to something, then this means that the decision has already been made. Unless and until you are fully committed to something, you will always end up being a victim of all the external circumstances in life. If you just rely on your willpower, it is more likely that you will end up crumbling. You might think that you are doing better than what you actually are doing. You needn't rely on your willpower once you have given your 100% commitment. Regardless of the circumstances, your decision has been made. It is all about being proactive instead of being reactive.

Well, improving your level of self-esteem does sound good. However, are you wondering how you can do so? In this chapter, you will learn about a couple of practical tips that you can make use of for improving as well as maintaining your self-esteem. So, read on to learn more.

Step 1: It's time to stop your inner critic

> *"I think everybody's weird. We should all celebrate our individuality and not be embarrassed or ashamed of it."*
> *– Johnny Depp*

You can start working on developing your self-esteem by learning to handle and replace your inner critic with something positive and encouraging. You are your worst critic, and if you let your inner critic work overtime, your self-esteem is bound to take a beating. It does spur you on to complete things on time or to do things that will earn you acceptance of those around you. However, listening to it all the time will damage your self-esteem.

Your inner critic keeps shouting all sorts of negative thoughts like "you are lazy, now start working", "you aren't good at what you are doing, someone will find that, and you will be thrown out", "you aren't good enough, your friend/colleague/partner is better", and so on. All these bitter thoughts will make you negative in life. However, you don't have to listen to it all. You can minimize this critical voice, and you can replace it with positive thoughts. You are the only one that has the power to change your perception of yourself. You can do this by simply asking the critic to stop whenever you feel the negativity creeping in. You can come up with a stop-word/phrase. Whenever you feel something negative coming your way, shout, "STOP" in your mind. Or how about a simple "Oh no, no, we aren't going there!" Or anything else that you can think of. Anything that will stop the inner critic from getting a hold of your thoughts. If you let yourself become too critical of your thoughts and actions, all the time, you will just make yourself feel inadequate. Once you stop yourself from criticizing yourself too harshly, you can refocus your thoughts towards something constructive. You can start planning for the rest of the week, or even think about your next meal.

Motivating yourself and ignoring your inner critic at times will keep you going.

Step 2: Better motivation habits

"Most of the shadows of this life are caused by standing in one's sunshine."
– Ralph Waldo Emerson

Your inner critic can be quite hateful at times, and that kind of self-hatred isn't going to do you any good. You can make your inner critic less useful, weaken the negative voice, and motivate yourself by developing healthier motivation habits. Your inner critic might at times drive you to perform better. However, more often than not, the critic is too critical. So, you can develop healthier motivation habits by reminding yourself of all the benefits that you can reap by achieving a goal and by refocusing your energy on things that you enjoy. Keep thinking about all the positive things that you will get completing a task. You can write these benefits down and keep looking at it whenever you feel like your motivational levels are plummeting. For instance, if your goal is to lose weight and get in shape.

Then think about how good you will feel when you have reached your ideal weight and have more energy and stamina than you ever did. Make your visualization as specific and clear as you possibly can. Doing this will help you keep going.

Once you have made a list of all the positive points, place it in a place where it will be visible to you, like your fridge or the dressing table. Whenever you feel low on motivation, divert your attention towards something that you like. When you like something, you will automatically find the motivation to keep going. Ask yourself if whether the task at hand is something you like or not, and if it isn't thought of a possible way in which you can make it enjoyable. You can also use a reward as motivation. The reward needn't be anything fancy or elaborate. Maybe you can treat yourself to a cup of coffee if you complete your work on time.

Step 3: Give yourself a pep talk

> *"Your problem is you're... too busy holding onto your unworthiness."*
> *– Ram Dass*

You are your cheerleader! Don't forget that. You can give yourself a pep talk for two minutes every time you feel your self-esteem is taking a blow. It is a very simple and enjoyable habit to develop. If you just spend two minutes on yourself, every day if possible, you can see an improvement in yourself. Breathe in slow and deep; let your mind relax and think: "What are the three things I appreciate about myself?" Your answer could be anything like "I am funny, I am helpful, and I am a good listener." This simple exercise will make you realize your positive qualities. Learning to appreciate yourself is directly proportional to your self-esteem. These short dialogues can help you in developing your self-esteem, and over a period, you will be able to turn your negative thoughts into positive ones in no time. If you don't appreciate yourself, you cannot expect anyone else to either.

Step 4: Write down three things in the evening that you like about yourself

It might sound similar to the previous suggestion, and if you combine these two habits, you can give your self-esteem a healthy boost daily. Or instead of the method mentioned above, you can make this variation a daily habit. At the end of the day, whenever you can spare a couple of minutes, you can practice this habit. You need to ask yourself the same question you did from the previous section "what are the three things I appreciate about myself?" However, in this variation, you are supposed to write down your answer in a journal. You need to document your responses. When you write these things down, you always have the option of flipping through the pages and going through the wonderful things you have written about yourself. That will give your self-esteem a nice boost.

Step 5: Doing the right thing

"It is never too late to be what you might have been."
– George Eliot

When you know that you are doing the right thing and you truly believe in it, you start strengthening your self-esteem in this process. The "right thing" doesn't have to be anything significant. Even something as simple as getting up from the couch and exercising will do. Instead of judging someone immediately, take the time to understand their perspective. Or to stop wallowing in self-pity and being grateful for the things you have will make you feel better. Doing the right thing might not always be easy, and it might not even be easy to know what the right thing is. However, focusing on it and doing your best makes a huge difference. It can help you in changing the outcome of a situation and how you think about yourself. A simple tip that you can make use of for doing the right is: taking action early in the day. For instance, complimenting someone, working out in the morning, or even having a healthy breakfast. Doing a good thing in the morning will set the tone for the rest of the day.

"Self-pity gets you nowhere. One must have the adventurous daring to accept oneself as a bundle of possibilities and undertake the most interesting game in the world making the most of one's best."
– Harry Emerson Fosdick

Step 6: Stop chasing perfectionism

Chasing perfectionism can be your downfall. Perfectionism is a double-edged sword. If you concentrate too much on it, it will leave you immobilized, and you wouldn't be able to take any action. The fear of not living up to some standard you have set for yourself will be your downfall. This fear leads to procrastination, and you will never be able to achieve what you want to, and your self-esteem is going to sink. Or maybe you do take some action, but that action is never satisfactory. Your dissatisfaction with yourself will make you feel more negative towards yourself. All this negativity will prevent you from achieving your goals, and it will hurt your self-esteem along the way. Perfection isn't attainable; so let it go. You are never going to be perfect, and no one is ever going to be perfect. There is no such thing as the perfect body, perfect life, perfect relationship, perfect job, or anything of that sort. Perfection is all relative and subjective. Its definition changes from one individual to another. We all tend to revel in the idea of perfection that society has created. It is just an idea that doesn't exist.

You can overcome perfectionism by doing a couple of simple things. Instead of aiming for perfection all the time, you can perhaps settle for good enough. When you start chasing perfection, there rarely is an end to it. So, opt for good enough. However, this shouldn't be your excuse to slack off. It is important that you understand what good enough is and stop once you have reached that stage. Life isn't like a movie and perfectionism is a myth. Stop chasing it and save yourself and your loved ones from getting hurt. Stop daydreaming about perfection. Your expectations of perfection will always clash with reality, and this can damage your personal and professional life. So, snap out of your daydream and start being practical. Learn to celebrate your accomplishments and start celebrating them. Acknowledge the things you have achieved and appreciate their value. Don't try to devalue your achievements by saying something like "oh that? Anyone can do it, and it was very easy for me". You can start maintaining a journal for recording all your accomplishments. Whenever you feel dejected, you can go through the list of amazing things you have accomplished. You can update your journal on a daily or weekly basis. Start by setting small goals for yourself and make it a point to achieve those goals. Once you have achieved those goals, you can record them in your journal.

Step 7: Mistakes and failures should be dealt with positively

If you step out of your comfort zone, if you try working on something that is meaningful to you, you will likely stumble along the way. It is okay to stumble and fall. Everyone goes through these things. However, it is essential to keep going without giving up, and that's what counts. Mistakes and failures are a part of life, and all those who ever did something that mattered to them did go through all these things. It is important to celebrate your success, but it is equally important to learn something from your failures as well. Mistakes and failures are just minor setbacks, and they are opportunities to learn and grow. Only when you push yourself will you know what you are truly capable of. Deal with mistakes and failures positively and whenever you stumble or fall, try this:

Instead of kicking yourself mentally, ask how your friend, parent, or partner supports you in a situation like the one you are in? You are your best friend, and you don't have to depend on anyone else to make you feel good about yourself. Think about the advice someone who cared for you would have given you and do that. It will stop you from reeling in despair and will allow you to take a more constructive route towards dealing with mistakes and failures. Another way in which you can be more constructive is by focusing on the upside. Every situation presents you with certain opportunities. All you need to do is look for the positivity in it, instead of concentrating on the negatives. A simple change in the way you look at things can make you feel better about a given situation. When you start treating a failure or a mistake as a bump along the way, you will feel better about yourself, and your self-esteem will thank you.

Step 8: Be kind towards others

When you start being compassionate towards others, you will start being more helpful to yourself as well. The way you treat others is how they will treat you. So, why don't you start concentrating on being kind? For instance, when someone wants to vent, lend him your ear! Just listen to him. Maybe you can hold the door open for the next person. Let someone else switch into your lane while driving. When someone feels uncertain or deflated, try saying something was encouraging to him. You can spend a couple of minutes to help someone else.

Step 9: Trying something new

When you try something new, you tend to challenge yourself. You are forcing yourself to step out of your comfort zone to do something new. When you do this, your opinion of yourself soars. You might or might not have been successful, but at least you tried, and that's way better than not doing anything. You can be appreciative of the courage it took to do something new. You can get out of the rut you were in. So, keep stepping out of your comfort zone. Don't expect anything and just concentrate on the task at hand. Once you have done this, keep doing it until you can improve your performance. It might be scary and uncomfortable to step out of your comfort zone, so start by taking small steps. Once you get into the groove of doing things, you will feel better.

Step 10: Stop comparing

When you start comparing your life, yourself, and what you have to others and what they have, you are creating a self-destructive habit. You can never win. There will always be someone who is better than you at something or the other. There will always be people ahead of you. The habit of comparing yourself to others is quite terrible, and you will never get anything good out of it. For instance, maybe you have 300 followers on Instagram, and your friend has 3000 followers. Your colleague might have a bigger house than you and probably drives a nicer car. The feeling of jealousy will make you feel bad about yourself. It might not be an easy habit to stop, but try to stop yourself from comparing as much as you can. You are your competition. Try to be the best version of yourself and don't waste your time by indulging in unfair comparisons. You aren't going to get anything out of it, and all that will happen is that you will feel bad and your self-esteem is going to be dented. These comparisons are unfair because you don't know what others are going through. The age-old adage of "the grass always looks greener on the other side" is true. Your friend might be lonely regardless of the fact that she has 3000 followers, and your colleague might be trapped in a loveless marriage regardless of the nicer house he lives in. Try to replace this habit with something that isn't destructive. Look how much you have progressed. Think of all the things you have managed to accomplish instead of comparing yourself to others. Start focusing on yourself and the results will surprise you.

30-day plan

You can follow a simple plan for improving your self-esteem within 30 days. The plan has been divided into two parts: daily and weekly basis.

Daily Basis

You need to take some time out of your daily schedule for practicing the steps that you have read about in this book.

Morning: Every morning, take a couple of minutes and read positive affirmations that will help in providing you with a positive outlook. If you are looking for some inspiration, then you can make use of the affirmations that have been mentioned in the next chapter.

At work: Take a minute or two and repeat a few positive affirmations. Whenever you feel low, or you feel like you are stuck, fill your mind with positive thoughts. Think about all the good that you have accomplished so far.

Evening: Start maintaining a journal. You need to record your daily experiences in it. Start by writing down the things you accomplished in the day, the moments when you felt happy or sad, the affirmations you used, and whether they helped or not.

Weekly basis

Make it a point to evaluate your progress every week. Follow this for four weeks without any deviations.

Read the journal: Go through the journal and see if you can identify a pattern of your behavior. There might have been particular instances or incidents that would have triggered a similar kind of reaction from you. Also, your mood might elevate or dip at different times during the day. When you notice a pattern, you can take corrective action to rectify it.

Evaluate the affirmations: Go through the affirmations that you have been using. Notice if you feel like there is a positive change in you or not. If you feel like a change needs to be made, then make the necessary changes. Feel free to tweak the affirmations to make the most of them.

Repeat the affirmations: Once you have tweaked the affirmations, repeat them a couple of times.

Bonus Chapter One: Affirmations

"Never bend your head. Always hold it high. Look the world straight in the face."
– Helen Keller

An affirmation is a positive thought or saying that will help in achieving a positive outlook towards your life. In this chapter, you will find different affirmations that you can make use of in different aspects of your life.

Affirmations for improving self-esteem

- I am skilled, smart, and capable.
- I have faith in myself.
- I am aware of the good qualities I possess.
- I see the best in myself and those around me.
- I surround myself with people who bring out the best in me.
- I let go of all undesirable thoughts and feelings about myself.
- I am always growing and developing, and I love myself.

Affirmations for relationship

- I love my son/daughter, and I get along fine with him/her.

- I have nothing but infinite and unconditional love towards my partner.
- I respect and cherish my parents, partners, and friends.

Affirmations for developing performance at school or university

- I am a model student. My teachers are incredible and knowledgeable. I love them and their teaching.
- I love learning something new every day.
- I will give my best while studying.

Affirmations for sports

- I can do this. I have trained hard for this.
- I trust myself and all the practice I have had.
- I can hit any pitch.

Affirmations for improving performance for workplace

- I have a great rapport with my colleagues and my boss.
- I am happy with the work I do, and it interests me.
- I am glad that the work I do, contributes towards the betterment of society.

- I am good at what I do, and I enjoy it.

Affirmations for improving your dating life

- I am beautiful and desirable.
- I deserve to be treated well and loved.
- I am fun, sexy, and charismatic.
- I am capable, confident, and wonderful to talk to.

Affirmations for reaching goals

- I have written down my goals, and I keep reviewing them.
- I can achieve my goals if I work hard.
- I'm firmly on the path to achievement and success.
- I can accomplish what I've set out to do.

Conclusion

I would like to thank you once again for purchasing this book. Self-esteem is the regard you have for yourself, and like any other aspect of your life, you can work on improving your self-esteem as well. The first step towards improving your self-esteem is to understand whether you have high or low self-esteem. Once you do this, you can start taking corrective action immediately. Self-esteem is the secret ingredient that has the power of transforming your life!

By making use of the simple steps and tips mentioned in this book, you can use your vulnerabilities as a source of power. You can start designing a new self-image of yourself that supports your goals and ambitions. You need to realize that you can be whoever you want to be. It all depends on your perceptions, and you are the only one who has the power to change it. You can reinvent yourself and create a life for yourself that you always wanted. The key to happiness and success lies in your hand!

Thank you and all the best!

www.ingramcontent.com/pod-product-compliance
Lightning Source LLC
Chambersburg PA
CBHW052124110526
44592CB00013B/1742